OMB SEQUESTRATION PREVIEW REPORT
TO THE PRESIDENT AND CONGRESS
FOR FISCAL YEAR 2014
AND
OMB REPORT TO THE CONGRESS
ON THE JOINT COMMITTEE
REDUCTIONS FOR FISCAL YEAR 2014

April 10, 2013

Original Version, superseded by *Corrected Version*

TABLE OF CONTENTS

Page

Transmittal Letter v

OMB Sequestration Preview Report to the President and Congress for Fiscal Year 2014

Introduction 1

Discretionary Sequestration Preview Report 3

OMB Report to the Congress on the Joint Committee Reductions for Fiscal Year 2014

Report 11

Appendix 17

GENERAL NOTES

1. All years referred to are fiscal years unless otherwise noted.

2. Details in the tables and text may not add to totals due to rounding.

April 10, 2013

The President
The White House
Washington, DC 20500

Dear Mr. President:

Enclosed please find two Office of Management and Budget (OMB) reports on sequestration: the *OMB Sequestration Preview Report to the President and Congress for Fiscal Year 2014* and the *OMB Report to the Congress on the Joint Committee Reductions for Fiscal Year 2014.* The reports have been prepared consistent with the requirements of the Balanced Budget and Emergency Deficit Control Act of 1985 (BBEDCA), as amended.

The *OMB Sequestration Preview Report to the President and Congress for Fiscal Year 2014* is the first of the three required reports on discretionary sequestration for fiscal year (FY) 2014 under section 254 of BBEDCA. It sets forth estimates of the applicable discretionary spending limits ("caps") for each category for the current year and each subsequent year through 2021. This includes any adjustments based on current law and adjustments due to changes in concepts and definitions. The report also provides a summary of the President's proposed and anticipated changes to the discretionary caps.

The *OMB Report to the Congress on the Joint Committee Reductions for Fiscal Year 2014* provides OMB's estimates of the reductions for FY 2014 required by section 251A of BBEDCA. This report provides calculations of the amounts by which the discretionary caps specified in section 251(c) of BBEDCA are required to be lowered for FY 2014 and a listing of the reductions required in FY 2014 for each non-exempt budget account with direct spending.

These reductions are triggered by the failure of the Joint Select Committee on Deficit Reduction to propose, and the Congress to enact, comprehensive and responsible deficit reduction legislation to achieve the savings targets enacted in August 2011 as part of the Budget Control Act (BCA). The Administration has no discretion in the calculation and allocation of the reductions. Instead, the reductions have been calculated pursuant to the requirements specified in the BCA. In FY 2014, the law requires the lowering of the discretionary caps by $91 billion and the sequestration of $18 billion in direct spending. Specifically, the defense discretionary cap will be reduced by $54 billion and the nondefense discretionary cap will be reduced by $37 billion. Additionally, OMB calculates that the sequestration of non-exempt direct spending requires reductions of 2.0 percent to non-exempt Medicare spending, 7.3 percent to other non-exempt nondefense mandatory programs, and 9.8 percent to non-exempt defense mandatory programs.

OMB is required by law to issue these reports. However, the reductions calculated in these reports demonstrate the need to enact a comprehensive deficit reduction plan to replace the Joint Committee reductions and set an appropriate level of spending in FY 2014 to support economic growth and job creation and provide for critical government services. The proposals set forth in the FY 2014 Budget reflect the tough choices that must be made. The Administration stands ready to work with the Congress to enact comprehensive deficit reduction legislation that replaces the blunt Joint Committee reductions with responsible, balanced deficit reduction and puts the Nation on a sound long-term fiscal path.

Sincerely,

Jeffrey D. Zients
Acting Director

Enclosure

Identical Letter Sent to The Honorable Joseph R. Biden
and The Honorable John A. Boehner

INTRODUCTION

The Budget Control Act of 2011 (BCA), *P.L. 112–25*, amended the Balanced Budget and Emergency Deficit Control Act of 1985 (BBEDCA) by reinstating limits ("caps") on discretionary budget authority, which expired after 2002. The 2013 and 2014 limits were revised further by the American Taxpayer Relief Act of 2012 (ATRA), *P.L. 112–240*. Section 254 of BBEDCA requires OMB to issue a sequestration preview report with the President's budget submission. This preview report, the first of the three required sequestration reports for 2014, provides the status of the discretionary caps for the current year and each year thereafter through 2021 as of the end of the second session of the 112th Congress based on current law, including further adjustments made to the current year (2013) caps in the *OMB Final Sequestration Report for FY 2013*, the release of which was delayed by ATRA. This report also includes adjustments to the budget year (2014) caps that are based on the reductions required pursuant to section 251A of BBEDCA as calculated in the *OMB Report to the Congress on the Joint Committee Reductions for Fiscal Year 2014*. Finally, this report details the President's proposals to restore the reductions in the 2014 caps to the levels agreed to in the bipartisan BCA as amended by ATRA.

Throughout each session of the Congress, OMB is required to monitor compliance with the discretionary spending limits. Within seven working days of enactment of an appropriations bill, OMB reports its estimates of the total discretionary budget authority and outlays provided by the legislation. If the bill provides additional appropriations for the current year, OMB also determines at that time whether the additional budget authority would cause total discretionary appropriations to exceed the caps. OMB makes the same determination for the budget year at the end of each session of the Congress. Appropriations that OMB estimates exceed the caps trigger an across-the-board reduction (or sequestration) to eliminate the excess spending. The law does not require that the Congress appropriate the full amount available under the discretionary caps.

OMB will issue a sequestration update report in August that will provide a mid-year status update on the caps and enacted appropriations, as well as a preview estimate of the 2014 adjustment for disaster funding. OMB will issue a final sequestration report for 2014 after the end of this congressional session that will contain final estimates of enacted appropriations and any adjustments to the discretionary caps. If it is determined that a breach has occurred, the final report will also include a Presidential Order for implementing a sequestration of non-exempt discretionary accounts to eliminate the breach as calculated by OMB. This sequestration, were it to occur, would be distinct from the Joint Committee sequestration pursuant to Section 251A of BBEDCA. As required by BBEDCA, OMB's estimates in each seven-day-after report and each sequestration report, including this report, are made using the same economic and technical assumptions underlying the President's Budget. In addition, each of these reports will contain comparisons between OMB's estimates and estimates from the Congressional Budget Office, where appropriate, and an explanation of any differences between those estimates.

DISCRETIONARY SEQUESTRATION PREVIEW REPORT

Discretionary programs are funded annually through the appropriations process. BBEDCA, as amended by the BCA and ATRA, limits—or caps—budget authority available for discretionary programs each year through 2021. Section 251 of BBEDCA originally specified for 2012 and 2013 separate "security" and "nonsecurity" categories for discretionary programs. The security category includes discretionary appropriations associated with agency budgets for the Department of Defense, the Department of Homeland Security, the Department of Veterans Affairs, the National Nuclear Security Administration, the Intelligence Community Management Account, and all discretionary budget accounts in budget function 150 (international affairs). The nonsecurity category includes all budget accounts that do not fall into the security category. After 2013, section 251 specified a single category for all discretionary spending referred to as the "discretionary" category.

Section 302 of the BCA provided for revisions to the caps if legislation proposed by the Joint Select Committee on Deficit Reduction to reduce the deficit by more than $1.2 trillion was not enacted by January 15, 2012. Because such legislation was not enacted by this date, the section 302 revisions to the caps were triggered and reflected in the _OMB Final Sequestration Report for FY 2012_, issued on January 18, 2012.

As required by law, the security category was redefined to include only the discretionary programs in the defense budget function (050) (the "defense" category), which mainly consists of the Department of Defense and significant portions of agency budgets for the Department of Energy (including the National Nuclear Security Administration) and the Federal Bureau of Investigation. The nonsecurity category was redefined to consist of all discretionary programs not in the security category—essentially all non-defense (non-050) budget functions (the "non-defense" category). The defense and non-defense categories were put in place for 2013 through 2021, replacing the overall discretionary category for those years. While the separate caps were adjusted to reflect the redefinitions, the total amount of discretionary funding remained unchanged. However, section 901(d) of ATRA reinstated the original security and nonsecurity categories for 2013 only and reduced the caps by $4 billion, split evenly between the security and nonsecurity categories. ATRA also lowered the 2014 caps by $8 billion, split evenly between the defense and non-defense categories, and effectively left intact the defense/non-defense cap framework for 2014 through 2021.

Table 1 summarizes the history of changes that have occurred to the discretionary caps since their reinstatement and subsequent redefinition in the BCA and ATRA. Table 1 also summarizes the changes to these caps proposed in the 2014 Budget, which are discussed in more detail in the proposed and anticipated adjustments section below.

Current Law Adjustments to Discretionary Caps

BBEDCA permits certain adjustments to the discretionary caps. After consultation with the Congressional Budget Office and the Congressional Budget Committees, section 251(b)(1) allows for adjustments due to changes in concepts and definitions in this report. Section 251(b)(2) also authorizes certain adjustments after the enactment of appropriations. At this time, OMB includes no change to the caps for concepts and definitions or adjustments pursuant to section 251(b)(2).

Pursuant to section 251A of BBEDCA, reductions are required to the discretionary caps due to the failure of the Congress to enact sufficient deficit reduction legislation. OMB has no discretion in the calculation and allocation of the reductions. Instead, OMB must calculate the reductions pursuant to the requirements specified in the BCA. The reductions for 2013 were implemented by a

Table 1. OVERVIEW OF CHANGES TO DISCRETIONARY SPENDING LIMITS AND THE PRESIDENT'S PROPOSED LIMITS IN THE 2014 BUDGET

(Discretionary budget authority in billions of dollars)

	2012	2013	2014	2015	2016	2017	2018	2019	2020	2021	2022	2023
Original limits set in Title I of the Budget Control Act of 2011:												
Security Category	684.0	686.0	N/A	N/A	N/A	N/A	N/A	N/A	N/A	N/A	N/A	N/A
Nonsecurity Category	359.0	361.0	N/A	N/A	N/A	N/A	N/A	N/A	N/A	N/A	N/A	N/A
Discretionary Category	N/A	N/A	1,066.0	1,086.0	1,107.0	1,131.0	1,156.0	1,182.0	1,208.0	1,234.0	N/A	N/A
Enacted adjustments pursuant to section 251(b)(2) of BBEDCA:												
OCO/GWOT:												
Security Category	+126.5	+98.7	....	....	....	....	....	....	....	....	N/A	N/A
Emergency Requirements:												
Security Category	....	+7.0	....	....	....	....	....	....	....	....	N/A	N/A
Nonsecurity Category	....	+34.6	....	....	....	....	....	....	....	....	N/A	N/A
Program Integrity:												
Nonsecurity Category	+0.5	+0.5	....	....	....	....	....	....	....	....	N/A	N/A
Disaster Relief:												
Security Category	+6.4	+11.8	....	....	....	....	....	....	....	....	N/A	N/A
Nonsecurity Category	+4.1	....	....	....	....	....	....	....	....	....	N/A	N/A
Redefinition of limits pursuant to section 251A of BBEDCA:												
Security Category	....	-686.0	N/A	N/A	N/A	N/A	N/A	N/A	N/A	N/A	N/A	N/A
Nonsecurity Category	....	-361.0	N/A	N/A	N/A	N/A	N/A	N/A	N/A	N/A	N/A	N/A
Discretionary Category	N/A	N/A	-1,066.0	-1,086.0	-1,107.0	-1,131.0	-1,156.0	-1,182.0	-1,208.0	-1,234.0	N/A	N/A
Defense Category	N/A	+546.0	+556.0	+566.0	+577.0	+590.0	+603.0	+616.0	+630.0	+644.0	N/A	N/A
Non-Defense Category	N/A	+501.0	+510.0	+520.0	+530.0	+541.0	+553.0	+566.0	+578.0	+590.0	N/A	N/A
Adjustments pursuant to section 901(d) of the ATRA:												
Security Category	....	+684.0	N/A	N/A	N/A	N/A	N/A	N/A	N/A	N/A	N/A	N/A
Nonsecurity Category	....	+359.0	N/A	N/A	N/A	N/A	N/A	N/A	N/A	N/A	N/A	N/A
Defense Category	N/A	-546.0	-4.0	....	....	....	....	....	....	....	N/A	N/A
Non-Defense Category	N/A	-501.0	-4.0	....	....	....	....	....	....	....	N/A	N/A
Joint Select Committee on Deficit Reduction Enforcement:												
Defense Category	N/A	....	-53.9	....	....	....	....	....	....	....	N/A	N/A
Non-Defense Category	N/A	....	-37.2	....	....	....	....	....	....	....	N/A	N/A
Revised Limits Included in the OMB Preview Report:												
Security Category	816.9	801.5	N/A	N/A	N/A	N/A	N/A	N/A	N/A	N/A	N/A	N/A
Nonsecurity Category	363.5	394.1	N/A	N/A	N/A	N/A	N/A	N/A	N/A	N/A	N/A	N/A
Discretionary Category	N/A	N/A	N/A	N/A	N/A	N/A	N/A	N/A	N/A	N/A	N/A	N/A
Defense Category	N/A	....	498.1	566.0	577.0	590.0	603.0	616.0	630.0	644.0	N/A	N/A
Non-Defense Category	N/A	....	468.8	520.0	530.0	541.0	553.0	566.0	578.0	590.0	N/A	N/A
President's Proposed Changes to Discretionary Limits in the 2014 Budget:												
Restore limits to the bipartisan agreement in the ATRA:												
Defense Category	N/A	N/A	+53.9	....	....	....	....	....	....	....	N/A	N/A
Non-Defense Category	N/A	N/A	+37.2	....	....	....	....	....	....	....	N/A	N/A
New Budget Proposals:												
Reduce limits and extend them to 2023:												
Defense Category	N/A	N/A	....	....	....	-4.0	-8.0	-12.0	-16.0	-20.0	+634.0	+644.0
Non-Defense Category	N/A	N/A	....	....	....	-4.0	-8.0	-12.0	-16.0	-20.0	+578.0	+587.0
Reclassification of General Fund Transportation rail accounts:												
Non-Defense Category	N/A	N/A	-1.5	-1.5	-1.5	-1.5	-1.6	-1.6	-1.6	-1.7	-1.7	-1.7
Reductions of base program integrity funding for shift to mandatory:												
Non-Defense Category	N/A	N/A	....	-0.6	-0.6	-0.6	-0.6	-0.6	-0.6	-0.6	-0.6	-0.6
New program integrity adjustments for IRS and UI:												
Non-Defense Category	N/A	N/A	+0.4	+0.8	+1.1	+1.4	+1.7	+1.7	+1.7	+1.8	+1.8	+1.9
Anticipated adjustments pursuant to section 251(b)(2) of BBEDCA:												
OCO/GWOT:												
Defense Category	N/A	N/A	+88.5	....	....	....	....	....	....	....	....	....
Non-Defense Category	N/A	N/A	+3.8	+37.3	+37.3	+37.3	+37.3	+37.3	+37.3	+37.3	....	....
Disaster Relief:												
Non-Defense Category	N/A	N/A	+5.8	....	....	....	....	....	....	....	....	....
President's proposed limits in the 2014 Budget:												
Security Category	816.9	801.5	N/A	N/A	N/A	N/A	N/A	N/A	N/A	N/A	N/A	N/A
Nonsecurity Category	363.5	394.1	N/A	N/A	N/A	N/A	N/A	N/A	N/A	N/A	N/A	N/A
Discretionary Category	N/A	N/A	N/A	N/A	N/A	N/A	N/A	N/A	N/A	N/A	N/A	N/A
Defense Category	N/A	N/A	640.5	566.0	577.0	586.0	595.0	604.0	614.0	624.0	634.0	644.0
Non-Defense Category	N/A	N/A	514.6	556.0	566.2	573.5	581.8	590.8	598.8	606.8	577.5	586.6

N/A = Not Applicable

sequestration ordered on March 1, 2013. The 2014 reductions for discretionary spending are achieved through reductions to the discretionary caps. As explained in the *OMB Report to the Congress on the Joint Committee Reductions for Fiscal Year 2014*, the defense cap is required to be reduced by $53,918 million and the non-defense cap is required to be reduced by $37,158 million. These adjustments are made to the current law caps in Table 2. In subsequent preview reports, OMB will be required to implement reductions to the discretionary caps for future years unless legislation is enacted to cancel the Joint Committee reductions. Because those reductions are not required at this time and would

Table 2. PREVIEW REPORT DISCRETIONARY SPENDING LIMITS UNDER CURRENT LAW
(Discretionary budget authority in millions of dollars)

	2013	2014	2015	2016	2017	2018	2019	2020	2021
SECURITY CATEGORY									
Final Sequestration Report Spending Limit.........	801,503	N/A	N/A	N/A	N/A	N/A	N/A	N/A	N/A
No changes									
Preview Report Spending Limit.........	801,503	N/A	N/A	N/A	N/A	N/A	N/A	N/A	N/A
NONSECURITY CATEGORY									
Final Sequestration Report Spending Limit.........	394,110	N/A	N/A	N/A	N/A	N/A	N/A	N/A	N/A
No changes									
Preview Report Spending Limit.........	394,110	N/A	N/A	N/A	N/A	N/A	N/A	N/A	N/A
DISCRETIONARY CATEGORY									
Final Sequestration Report Spending Limit.........	N/A	N/A	N/A	N/A	N/A	N/A	N/A	N/A	N/A
No changes									
Preview Report Spending Limit.........	N/A	N/A	N/A	N/A	N/A	N/A	N/A	N/A	N/A
DEFENSE (OR "REVISED SECURITY") CATEGORY									
Final Sequestration Report Spending Limit.........	N/A	552,000	566,000	577,000	590,000	603,000	616,000	630,000	644,000
Joint Committee Enforcement Reductions pursuant to section 251A of BBEDCA: Defense Cap Reduction for 2014.........	N/A	-53,918	....	....	....	....	....	....	....
Preview Report Spending Limit.........	N/A	498,082	566,000	577,000	590,000	603,000	616,000	630,000	644,000
NON-DEFENSE (OR "REVISED NONSECURITY") CATEGORY									
Final Sequestration Report Spending Limit.........	N/A	506,000	520,000	530,000	541,000	553,000	566,000	578,000	590,000
Joint Committee Enforcement Reductions pursuant to section 251A of BBEDCA: Non-Defense Cap Reduction for 2014.........	N/A	-37,158	....	....	....	....	....	....	....
Preview Report Spending Limit.........	N/A	468,842	520,000	530,000	541,000	553,000	566,000	578,000	590,000
TOTAL DISCRETIONARY SPENDING									
2013 Budget Preview Report, Total Discretionary Spending.........	1,047,000	1,066,000	1,086,000	1,107,000	1,131,000	1,156,000	1,182,000	1,208,000	1,234,000
2013 Final Sequestration Report, Total Discretionary Spending.........	1,195,613	1,058,000	1,086,000	1,107,000	1,131,000	1,156,000	1,182,000	1,208,000	1,234,000
2014 Preview Report, Total Discretionary Spending.........	1,195,613	966,924	1,086,000	1,107,000	1,131,000	1,156,000	1,182,000	1,208,000	1,234,000

N/A = Not Applicable

need to be recalculated based on the estimates of direct spending programs in future budgets, the discretionary defense and non-defense caps for 2015 through 2021 remain unadjusted at this point.

These reductions, especially when coupled with the cuts already in place for 2013, will be deeply destructive to national security, domestic investments, and core Government functions. The President believes that comprehensive deficit reduction is necessary to replace the Joint Committee reductions and set an appropriate level of discretionary spending in 2014 to support economic growth and job creation and provide for critical government services. As reflected in the proposals set forth in the President's 2014 Budget, including those specified in the next section, the President is willing to make tough choices. He stands ready to work with the Congress to enact comprehensive deficit reduction legislation that replaces the blunt Joint Committee reductions with responsible, balanced deficit reduction and puts the Nation on a sound long-term fiscal path.

Proposed and Anticipated Adjustments to Discretionary Caps

The President's Budget includes several proposals to revise the discretionary caps. The effects of these changes are reflected in Table 3. To accompany these proposals, the 2014 Budget proposes savings across the mandatory and revenue categories and, in the interest of reaching an agreement on a comprehensive deficit reduction package, reductions to the discretionary caps to replace the automatic reductions, restore the 2013 sequestration amounts, cancel the 2014 mandatory sequestration order, and adjust upward the 2014 defense and non-defense caps to the levels agreed to by the Congress in ATRA. In addition, the 2014 Budget proposes to extend the discretionary caps through 2023. These reductions to, and extensions of, the discretionary caps will achieve additional discretionary outlays savings of $200 billion over the next decade when compared to current law. These reductions are split between the defense and non-defense categories and are timed to take effect beginning in 2017 when the economy is projected to have fully recovered.

The President's Budget also includes proposed changes in concepts and definitions that would reclassify as mandatory two transportation accounts that are currently funded from the General Fund as part of its passenger rail reauthorization. These changes are also included on Table 3. Please see "Budgetary Treatment of Surface Transportation Infrastructure Funding" in the Budget Process chapter in the *Analytical Perspectives* volume of the President's 2014 Budget for a full discussion of the policy.

Section 251(b)(2) of BBEDCA allows for adjustment of the discretionary caps provided that certain conditions are met and/or specific designations are provided. Several proposals included in the Budget, if enacted, would trigger these adjustments to the discretionary caps. The Budget also proposes to repeal two of these existing adjustments in order to shift funding for these purposes from discretionary to mandatory. These anticipated adjustments, shown in Table 3, include the following:

Emergency Appropriations and Overseas Contingency Operations / Global War on Terrorism (OCO / GWOT).—These adjustments are authorized by section 251(b)(2)(A) of BBEDCA and include funding for amounts that the Congress designates in law and the President subsequently so designates as being either an emergency requirement or for OCO/GWOT activities on an account-by-account basis. In 2013, $41,669 million was designated as an emergency requirement in response to Hurricane Sandy in the 2013 Disaster Relief Appropriations Act (*P.L. 113–2*). For 2014, however, the President's Budget does not propose any adjustments for emergency funding. 2013 appropriations for the Defense, Homeland Security, Military Construction and Veterans Affairs, and State and Foreign Operations

Table 3. PROPOSED CHANGES TO THE DISCRETIONARY SPENDING LIMITS
(Discretionary budget authority in millions of dollars)

	2013	2014	2015	2016	2017	2018	2019	2020	2021	2022	2023
SECURITY CATEGORY											
Preview Report Spending Limit....................................	801,503	N/A	N/A	N/A	N/A	N/A	N/A	N/A	N/A	N/A	N/A
No changes											
Proposed Spending Limit...	801,503	N/A	N/A	N/A	N/A	N/A	N/A	N/A	N/A	N/A	N/A
NONSECURITY CATEGORY											
Preview Report Spending Limit....................................	394,110	N/A	N/A	N/A	N/A	N/A	N/A	N/A	N/A	N/A	N/A
No changes											
Proposed Spending Limit...	394,110	N/A	N/A	N/A	N/A	N/A	N/A	N/A	N/A	N/A	N/A
DISCRETIONARY CATEGORY											
Preview Report Spending Limit....................................	N/A	N/A	N/A	N/A	N/A	N/A	N/A	N/A	N/A	N/A	N/A
No changes											
Proposed Spending Limit...	N/A	N/A	N/A	N/A	N/A	N/A	N/A	N/A	N/A	N/A	N/A
DEFENSE (OR "REVISED SECURITY") CATEGORY											
Preview Report Spending Limit....................................	N/A	498,082	566,000	577,000	590,000	603,000	616,000	630,000	644,000	N/A	N/A
Restore limits to the bipartisan agreement in section 901(d) of the ATRA.................................	N/A	+53,918	....	....	....	....	....	....	....	....	....
Reduce 2017-2021 caps and extend caps to 2023 for additional deficit reduction....................................	N/A	....	....	....	-4,000	-8,000	-12,000	-16,000	-20,000	+634,000	+644,000
Anticipated adjustments pursuant to Section 251(b)(2)(A) of BBEDCA for OCO/GWOT...................................	N/A	+88,482	....	....	....	....	....	....	....	....	....
Proposed Spending Limit...	N/A	640,482	566,000	577,000	586,000	595,000	604,000	614,000	624,000	634,000	644,000
NON-DEFENSE (OR "REVISED NONSECURITY") CATEGORY											
Preview Report Spending Limit....................................	N/A	468,842	520,000	530,000	541,000	553,000	566,000	578,000	590,000	N/A	N/A
Restore limits to the bipartisan agreement in section 901(d) of the ATRA.................................	N/A	+37,158	....	....	....	....	....	....	....	N/A	N/A
Reduce 2017-2021 caps and extend caps to 2023 for additional deficit reduction....................................	N/A	....	....	....	-4,000	-8,000	-12,000	-16,000	-20,000	+578,000	+587,000
Proposed change in concepts and definitions for reclassification of general fund Transportation rail accounts.............	N/A	-1,454	-1,482	-1,510	-1,539	-1,568	-1,598	-1,628	-1,659	-1,691	-1,722
Anticipated and Proposed Non-Defense Adjustments for the Final Sequestration Report:											
Anticipated adjustments pursuant to Section 251(b)(2)(A) of BBEDCA for OCO/GWOT...................................	N/A	+3,807	+37,283	+37,283	+37,283	+37,283	+37,283	+37,283	+37,283	....	....
Proposed reduction of base program integrity funding for CDRs and Redeterminations and HCFAC for shift to mandatory.....................	N/A	....	-584	-584	-584	-584	-584	-584	-584	-584	-584
Anticipated adjustments pursuant to Section 251(b)(2)(D) of BBEDCA for Disaster Relief...........................	N/A	+5,785	....	....	....	....	....	....	....	....	....
Proposed adjustments for Internal Revenue Service Program Integrity...	N/A	+412	+738	+1,030	+1,341	+1,662	+1,639	+1,650	+1,712	+1,773	+1,836
Proposed adjustments Unemployment Insurance Program Integrity...	N/A	+20	+25	+30	+35	+36	+37	+38	+39	+40	+41
Subtotal, Anticipated Non-Defense Adjustments......	N/A	+10,024	+38,046	+38,343	+38,659	+38,981	+38,959	+38,971	+39,034	+1,813	+1,877
Proposed Spending Limit...	N/A	514,570	555,980	566,249	573,536	581,829	590,777	598,759	606,791	577,538	586,571
TOTAL DISCRETIONARY SPENDING											
Final 2013 Sequestration Report, Total Discretionary Spending...................	1,195,613	1,058,000	1,086,000	1,107,000	1,131,000	1,156,000	1,182,000	1,208,000	1,234,000	N/A	N/A
Preview Report, Total Discretionary Spending...................	1,195,613	966,924	1,086,000	1,107,000	1,131,000	1,156,000	1,182,000	1,208,000	1,234,000	N/A	N/A
2014 Budget Proposed, Total Discretionary Spending...................	1,195,613	1,155,052	1,121,980	1,143,249	1,159,536	1,176,829	1,194,777	1,212,759	1,230,791	1,211,538	1,230,571

N/A = Not Applicable

subcommittees, all included in the Consolidated and Further Continuing Appropriations Act (*P.L. 113–6*), provided a total of $98,682 million (including rescissions) for OCO/GWOT purposes for 2013. For 2014, the President's Budget proposes to continue its 2013 Budget policy of placing a cumulative ceiling on the OCO/GWOT cap adjustment of $450 billion from 2013 to 2021. The President's Budget currently includes $92,289 million for OCO/GWOT activities for 2014, of which $3,807 million is for international programs. However, at the time the budget was printed, the Department of Defense (DOD) had not made final decisions about the pace of the drawdown in Afghanistan. Once DOD's OCO/GWOT needs for 2014 are determined, a budget amendment package will be transmitted subsequent to release of the Budget. For now, a placeholder for DOD that is equal to the 2013 Budget Request of $88,482 million is assumed in its place. The Budget also includes a cap adjustment of $37.3 billion for OCO/GWOT activities for each year in 2015 through 2021. The 2015-2021 levels reflect a placeholder of annual amounts for a total funding level for OCO/GWOT activities but do not reflect specific policy decisions as to how the funds will ultimately be allocated across those years. The budget amendment package for DOD will note if any changes to this assumption are necessary based on the final 2014 request. The DOD OCO/GWOT amounts are allocated to the defense category on Table 3, while the international and outyear placeholder amounts are allocated to the non-defense category.

Continuing Disability Reviews (CDRs) and Redeterminations.—Section 251(b)(2)(B) of BBEDCA authorizes adjustment of the caps by the amounts appropriated for CDRs and redeterminations. The maximum cap adjustment in each year is limited to the levels of budget authority specified in BBEDCA, provided that a base level of $273 million is provided for these purposes in the underlying appropriations bill before the adjustment. In the 2013 Consolidated and Further Continuing Appropriations Act (P.L. 113–6), $483 million was provided as a cap adjustment—an amount sufficient only to maintain activities at the 2012 level, and $268 million below the adjustment permitted under BBEDCA. The intent of this adjustment was to ensure sufficient resources for the Social Security Administration (SSA) to reduce improper payments and achieve tens of billions of dollars in deficit savings over the next ten years. However, the failure to provide the full level of adjustment authorized by BBEDCA and the uncertainty of annual appropriations for these activities has made these savings difficult to realize. As noted in *OMB's Final Sequestration Report for FY 2013*, the Congress will forgo approximately $1.9 billion in net deficit savings by not providing the full amount of the cap adjustment authorized for 2013. In order to better ensure these resources are provided, the Budget proposes instead to provide dedicated mandatory funding for these activities beginning in 2013. If mandatory funding is provided, the Budget proposes to eliminate the discretionary cap adjustment beginning in 2014 and to reduce the discretionary caps by the base funding for these activities beginning in 2015. The base appropriation of $273 million would still be provided for 2014 through discretionary appropriations. The "Program Integrity Funding" discussion in the President's Budget Reform Proposals section of the Budget Process chapter in the *Analytical Perspectives* volume of the Budget provides a complete description of this and other program integrity efforts along with OMB's methodology in determining their effectiveness.

Health Care Fraud and Abuse Control (HCFAC).—Section 251(b)(2)(C) of BBEDCA authorizes adjustment of the caps by amounts appropriated for HCFAC activities. The maximum HCFAC cap adjustment in each year is limited to the levels of budget authority specified in BBEDCA, provided that a base level of $311 million for these purposes is provided in the underlying appropriations bill before the adjustment. Because the 2013 Consolidated and Further Continuing Appropriations Act (P.L. 113–6) provided only $310 million of base funding (not including an across-the-board rescission in the final 2013 Act), an amount sufficient only to maintain activities at roughly their 2012 level, *OMB's Final Sequestration Report for FY 2013* did not include an adjustment for this funding. This is the second year in a row that the cap adjustment authorized by BBEDCA has not been provided, in whole or in part, for this program, which has led to an underfunding of efforts to prevent and reduce fraud and other improper payments in the Medicare and Medicaid programs. As noted in *OMB's Final Sequestration Report for FY 2013*, the Congress will forgo approximately $450 million in deficit savings by not fully funding the base appropriation and providing the full cap adjustment authorized for 2013. As with CDRs and redeterminations at SSA, the Budget proposes to repeal the discretionary cap adjustment for HCFAC, but starting in 2013 since the cap adjustment was not used, and provide dedicated mandatory funding for these activities beginning in that fiscal year. The Budget continues to seek the 2014 base appropriation of $311 million through discretionary appropriations, but after 2014 no discretionary funding would be provided for these activities and the discretionary non-defense caps are reduced accordingly. The "Program Integrity Funding" discussion in the President's Budget Reform Proposals section of the Budget Process chapter in the *Analytical Perspectives* volume of the 2014 Budget provides a for a fuller description of this and other program integrity efforts and OMB's methodology in determining their effectiveness.

Disaster Funding.—Section 251(b)(2)(D) of BBEDCA authorizes an adjustment to the caps for appropriations that are designated by the Congress as being for "disaster relief," which is defined as activities carried out pursuant to a determination under section 102(2) of the Robert T. Stafford Disaster Relief and Emergency Assistance Act (42 U.S.C. 5122(2)). BBEDCA sets a limit for the adjustment equal to the total of the average funding provided for disaster relief over the previous 10 years (excluding the highest and lowest years) plus any portion of the allowable adjustment (funding ceiling) for the previous year that was not appropriated (excluding the portion of the previous year's ceiling that was itself due to any unused amount from the year before). For the 2013 adjustment, OMB determined a preview estimate of $11,779 million. The full level of $11,779 million was provided for the Federal Emergency Management Agency's (FEMA's) Disaster Relief Fund (DRF) in one $6,400 million appropriation in the 2013 Consolidated and Further Continuing Appropriations Act (P.L. 113–6) and one $5,379 million appropriation in the 2013 Disaster Relief Appropriations Act (P.L. 113–2) in response to Hurricane Sandy. For 2014, OMB will present its preview estimate for disaster funding in its August update report. The 2014 Budget requests $5,785 million in funding in two accounts to be designated for disaster relief by the Congress: $5,626 million in FEMA's DRF to cover the costs of Presidentially-declared major disasters, including identified costs for previously declared catastrophic events and the predictable annual cost of non-catastrophic events expected to obligate in 2014, and $159 million in the Small Business Administration's Disaster Loans Program Account for administrative expenses. For the DRF, the request does not include additional funding for Hurricane Sandy, because the funding tail could not yet be determined at the time of allocation. However, it should be noted that this event will be reflected in the 2015 Budget. Both of these amounts are shown on Table 3 as an anticipated cap adjustment to the non-defense category. See "Disaster Relief Funding" in the President's Budget Reform Proposals section of the Budget Process chapter in the *Analytical Perspectives* volume of the 2014 Budget for a full description of this adjustment and the Administration's 2014 Request.

In addition to these adjustments, the 2014 Budget proposes to amend section 251(b)(2) of BBEDCA by adding two new discretionary cap adjustments related to program integrity efforts. These new adjustments are for tax enforcement, including tax compliance to address the Federal tax gap, via the Internal Revenue Service's (IRS) Enforcement and Operations Support accounts and the Alcohol and Tobacco Tax and Trade Bureau (TTB), and for in-person reemployment and eligibility assessments and unemployment insurance improper payment reviews by the Department of Labor. These new adjustments total $412 million for IRS and TTB and $20 million for the Department of Labor in 2014, and are included in Table 3 as anticipated adjustments to the proposed non-defense caps in all years. For more information on these new adjustments see the "Program Integrity Funding" section of the Budget Process chapter of the *Analytical Perspectives* volume of the 2014 Budget.

OMB REPORT TO THE CONGRESS ON THE JOINT COMMITTEE REDUCTIONS FOR FISCAL YEAR 2014

Due to the failure of the Joint Select Committee on Deficit Reduction to propose, and the Congress to enact, legislation to reduce the deficit by $1.2 trillion, the Balanced Budget and Emergency Deficit Control Act (BBEDCA), as amended, requires the Office of Management and Budget (OMB) to calculate reductions of fiscal year (FY) 2014 budgetary resources when the FY 2014 Budget is transmitted. This report provides OMB's calculations of the reductions to the discretionary spending limits ("caps") specified in section 251(c) of BBEDCA for FY 2014 and a listing of the FY 2014 reductions required through sequestration for each non-exempt budget account with direct spending.

OMB calculates that the Joint Committee reductions will lower the discretionary cap for the revised security (defense) category by $54 billion and for the revised non-security (nondefense) category by $37 billion. Additionally, the Joint Committee reductions require sequestration reductions to non-exempt direct spending of 2.0 percent to Medicare, 7.3 percent to other non-exempt nondefense mandatory programs, and 9.8 percent to non-exempt defense mandatory programs.

Calculation of Annual Reduction by Function Group

Under section 251A of BBEDCA, the failure of the Joint Select Committee on Deficit Reduction to propose, and the Congress to enact, legislation to reduce the deficit by $1.2 trillion triggers automatic reductions in FY 2014 through adjustments in the discretionary spending limits and a sequestration of direct spending. As shown in Table 1, the total amount of deficit reduction required is specified by formula in section 251A(3), starting with the total reduction of $1.2 trillion required for FY 2013 through FY 2021, deducting a specified 18 percent for debt service savings, and then dividing the result by 9 to calculate the annual reduction of $109 billion for each year from FY 2013 to FY 2021.[1] The annual reduction is split evenly between budget accounts in function 050 (defense function) and in all other functions (nondefense function), so that each function group will be reduced by $54.667 billion.

Table 1. CALCULATION OF TOTAL ANNUAL REDUCTION BY FUNCTION
(In billions of dollars)

Joint Committee required savings	1,200.000
Deduct debt service savings (18%)	−216.000
Net programmatic reductions	984.000
Divide by 9 to calculate annual reduction	109.333
Split 50/50 between defense and nondefense functions	54.667

Base for Allocating Reductions and Method of Reduction

The annual reduction is further allocated between discretionary and direct spending within each of the function groups. Once the reductions are allocated, separate methods are used to implement the reductions for discretionary appropriations and direct spending.

---

[1] The reduction for FY 2013 was revised by the American Taxpayer Relief Act of 2012, as explained in the OMB Report to the Congress on the Joint Committee Sequestration for Fiscal Year 2013, available at *http://www.whitehouse.gov/sites/default/files/omb/assets/legislative_reports/fy13ombjcsequestrationreport.pdf*.

Discretionary Reductions. The base for allocating reductions to discretionary appropriations is the discretionary spending limit for FY 2014 set forth in section 251(c)(3). The reductions are implemented by lowering the discretionary spending limits for the revised security (defense) category and the revised nonsecurity (nondefense) category.

Direct Spending Reductions. Pursuant to paragraphs (5) and (6) of section 251A, and consistent with section 6 of the Statutory Pay-As-You-Go Act of 2010, the base for allocating reductions to budget accounts with direct spending is the sum of the direct spending outlays in the budget year and the subsequent year that would result from sequestrable budgetary resources in FY 2014.

Estimates of sequestrable budgetary resources and outlays for budget accounts with direct spending are equal to the current law baseline amounts contained in the President's FY 2014 Budget, and include direct spending unobligated balances in the defense function[2] and Federal administrative expenses that would otherwise be exempt[3].

The majority of estimated direct spending unobligated balances in the defense function are in Department of Defense accounts. The Department of Defense estimates of unobligated balances as of October 1, 2013 are consistent with the estimates in the FY 2014 Budget.

For purposes of applying a sequestration under BBEDCA, "administrative expenses" for typical Government programs are defined as the object classes for personnel compensation, travel, transportation, communication, equipment, supplies, materials, and other services. For Government programs engaging in commercial, business-like activities, administrative expenses constitute overhead costs that are necessary to run a business, and not expenses that are directly tied to the production and delivery of goods or services.

The reductions to direct spending are implemented through sequestration of non-exempt budgetary resources. Pursuant to sections 251A(8), 255, and 256, most direct spending is exempt from sequestration or, in the case of the Medicare program and certain other health programs, is subject to a 2 percent limit on sequestration.

Defense Function Reduction

Steps 1 and 2 on Table 2 show the calculation of the reduction required for discretionary appropriations and direct spending within the defense function. Steps 3 and 4 on Table 2 reflect the implementation of the reductions calculated in steps 1 and 2 through an adjustment to the discretionary spending limit for the defense category and a sequestration of direct spending in the defense function.

The calculation of the reduction involves the following steps:

Step 1. Pursuant to section 251A(5), the total reduction of $54.667 billion is allocated proportionately between discretionary appropriations and direct spending. The total base is the sum of the FY 2014 discretionary spending limit for the defense category ($552 billion) and OMB's baseline estimates of sequestrable direct spending outlays ($7.673 billion) in the defense function in FY 2014 and FY 2015 from direct spending sequestrable resources in FY 2014. Discretionary appropriations comprise nearly 99 percent of the total base in the defense function.

Step 2. Total defense function spending must be reduced by $54.667 billion. As required by section 251A(5)(A), allocating the reduction based on the ratio of the discretion-

---

[2] Defense function unobligated balances are not exempt from sequestration pursuant to section 255(e) of BBEDCA.

[3] Under sections 251A(8) and 256(h) of BBEDCA, Federal administrative expenses are subject to sequestration "without regard to any exemption, exception, limitation, or special rule that is otherwise applicable."

ary spending limit to the total base (the sum of the defense discretionary spending limit and sequestrable direct spending) yields a $53.918 billion reduction required to be made to discretionary appropriations. Under section 251A(5)(B), the remaining $0.749 billion is the reduction required for budget accounts with direct spending.

The implementation of the reductions involves the following steps:

Step 3. As required by section 251A(7)(B), the discretionary spending limit for the defense category is lowered by the amount calculated in step 2, which results in a discretionary defense cap for FY 2014 of $498.082 billion.

Step 4. As required by section 251A(8), the percentage reduction for non-exempt direct spending is calculated by dividing the direct spending reduction amount ($0.749 billion) by the sequestrable budgetary resources ($7.673 billion) for budget accounts with direct spending, which yields a 9.8 percent sequestration for budget accounts with non-exempt direct spending.

Table 2. DEFENSE FUNCTION REDUCTION
(Dollars in billions)

	Discretionary	Direct Spending	Total
Calculation of Reduction:			
Step 1. Base for allocating reduction	552.000	7.673	559.673
Percentage allocation of reductions	98.63%	1.37%	
Step 2. Allocation of total reduction	53.918	0.749	54.667
Percentage allocation of reductions	98.63%	1.37%	
Implementation of Reduction:			
Step 3. Reduction in defense cap:			
Appropriations reduction required	−53.918		
Adjusted defense cap	498.082		
Step 4. Sequestration percentages calculation:			
Sequestrable base		7.673	
Sequestration percentage		9.8%	

Nondefense Function Reduction

Steps 1 through 3 on Table 3 show the calculation of the reduction required for discretionary appropriations and direct spending within all other functions besides 050 (nondefense function). The calculation is more complicated than the calculation for the defense function due to a two percent limit in the reduction of Medicare spending, a two percent limit in the reduction of community and migrant health centers, and a special rule for applying the reduction to student loans. Steps 4 and 5 on Table 3 reflect the implementation of the reductions calculated in steps 1 through 3 through an adjustment to the discretionary spending limit for the nondefense category and a sequestration of direct spending in the nondefense function.

The calculation of the reduction involves the following steps:

Step 1. Total spending in the nondefense function must be reduced by $54.667 billion. The portion of Medicare subject to the two percent limit is estimated to have combined FY 2014 and FY 2015 outlays of $557.870 billion from FY 2014 budgetary resources, so a two percentage point reduction would reduce outlays by $11.157 billion, leaving a reduction of $43.510 billion to be taken from discretionary appropriations and other direct spending in the nondefense function.

Step 2. Pursuant to section 251A(6), the remaining reduction of $43.510 billion is allocated proportionately between discretionary appropriations and other direct spending in the nondefense function. The base ($592.474 billion) is the sum of the FY 2014 discretionary spending limit for the nondefense category ($506.000 billion) and the remaining sequestrable direct spending base ($86.474 billion). The latter amount equals OMB's 2014 Budget baseline estimates of total sequestrable direct spending outlays in the nondefense function in FY 2014 and FY 2015 from direct spending sequestrable resources in FY 2014 ($644.344 billion) minus the portion of Medicare subject to the two percent limit ($557.870 billion). Discretionary appropriations account for 85.4 percent of the remaining base in the nondefense function, and direct spending accounts for 14.6 percent.

Applying these percentage allocations to the remaining required reduction for programs in the nondefense function yields the reduction for discretionary appropriations ($37.158 billion) and for remaining direct spending ($6.352 billion), following the procedures for allocating the sequestration contained in section 251A(6).

Step 3. The sequestration reduction for the mandatory portions of certain health programs is limited to two percent pursuant to sections 251A(8) and 256(e)(2). The portion of these programs subject to the two percent limit is estimated to have combined FY 2014 and FY 2015 outlays of $1.242 billion from FY 2014 budgetary resources, so a two percent reduction would reduce outlays by $0.025 billion. Deducting these savings from the non-Medicare direct spending reduction leaves $6.327 billion to be taken by a uniform percentage reduction of the remaining sequestrable direct spending of $85.232 billion in the nondefense function.

The implementation of the reductions involves the following steps:

Step 4. As required by section 251A(7)(B), the discretionary spending limit for the nondefense category is lowered by the amount calculated in step 2, which results in a discretionary nondefense cap for FY 2014 of $468.842 billion.

Step 5. The remaining reduction ($6.327 billion) to direct spending is applied as a uniform percentage reduction to the remaining budget accounts with sequestrable direct spending and by increasing student loan fees by the same uniform percentage, as specified in sections 251A(8) and 256(b). Each percentage point increase in the sequestration rate is estimated to result in $0.017 billion of savings in the direct student loan program. Solving simultaneously for the percentage that would achieve the remaining reduction when applied to both the remaining sequestrable direct spending ($85.232 billion) and to student loan fees yields a 7.3 percent reduction. This percentage reduction yields savings of $0.124 billion in the direct student loan program and $6.222 billion from the remaining budget accounts with non-exempt direct spending.

Table 3. NONDEFENSE FUNCTION REDUCTION
(Dollars in billions)

	Discretionary	Direct Spending	Total
Calculation of Reduction:			
1. Total reduction, excluding savings from Medicare 2% limit:			
Medicare base subject to 2% limit		557.870	
Total nondefense function reduction			54.667
Reduce Medicare by 2%			−11.157
Non-Medicare reduction amounts			43.510
2. Allocate non-Medicare reduction:			
Total base for allocating reduction	506.000	644.344	1,150.344
Exclude Medicare (portion subject to 2% limit)		−557.870	−557.870
Non-Medicare base	506.000	86.474	592.474
Percentage allocation of non-Medicare base	85.40%	14.60%	
Non-Medicare reduction amounts	37.158	6.352	43.510
Percentage allocation of non-Medicare reduction	85.40%	14.60%	
3. Savings from 2% limit on sequestration of other health programs*			
Other health programs sequestrable base		1.242	
Reduce other health programs by 2%		−0.025	
Implementation of Reduction:			
4. Reduction in nondefense cap:			
Appropriations reduction required	−37.158		
Adjusted nondefense cap	468.842		
5. Sequestration percentages calculation:			
Remaining reduction amounts		6.327	
Savings from uniform percentage reduction:			
From 7.3% increase in student loan fee		0.124	
From remaining sequestrable budget accounts		6.203	
Sequestrable base for uniform percentage reduction		85.232	
Sequestration percentage		7.3%	
Summary of Reductions:			
2% sequestration of Medicare		11.157	
2% limit on sequestration of other health programs		0.025	
Student loan fee increase		0.124	
Uniform percentage reduction		6.222	
Rounding		−0.019	
Total reduction	37.158	17.509	54.667

* Includes funding for community and migrant health centers, and for Indian health services.

Reductions to Discretionary Spending Limits

The reductions to the discretionary spending limits in both the defense and nondefense categories calculated in this report pursuant to section 251A of BBEDCA are reflected as adjustments to such limits in the OMB Discretionary Sequestration Preview Report, provided pursuant to section 254 of BBEDCA.

Direct Spending Reductions by Budget Account (Appendix)

The Appendix of this report sets forth the percentage and dollar amount of the reductions required for each budget account with sequestrable direct spending. Specifically, the Appendix shows the sequestrable budgetary resources in each budget account with direct spending, the percentage reduction required for each sequestrable budgetary resource, and the resulting reduction. For illustrative purposes only, the Appendix shows the application of the same percentage reduction to each type of budgetary resource within a budget account with direct spending. There is no requirement that sequestration be applied equally to each type of budgetary resource within a budget account. Section 256(k)(2) of BBEDCA requires that sequestration be applied equally at the program, project, and activity level.

APPENDIX:
DIRECT SPENDING SEQUESTRABLE BUDGETARY RESOURCES AND REDUCTIONS BY BUDGET ACCOUNT

(Fiscal year 2014; in millions of dollars)

Based on sections 251A, 255, and 256 of the Balanced Budget and Emergency
Deficit Control Act of 1985 (BBEDCA), as amended

Percentages Used:

9.8 percent – Defense mandatory

7.3 percent – Nondefense mandatory

2.0 percent – Medicare program and certain health programs

For illustrative purposes only, the Appendix shows the application of the same percentage reduction to each type of budgetary resource within a budget account. Pursuant to section 256(k)(2) of the Balanced Budget and Emergency Deficit Control Act of 1985, the sequestration must be applied equally at the program, project, and activity level, but need not be applied equally to each type of budgetary resource within a budget account.

Direct Spending Sequestrable Budgetary Resources and Reductions by Budget Account – FY 2014

(Amounts in millions)

Agency / Bureau / Account / Function / BEA Category / Budgetary Resource	Sequestrable BA Amount	Sequester Percentage	Sequester Amount
Legislative Branch			
Senate			
001-05-0188 Congressional Use of Foreign Currency, Senate			
Nondefense Mandatory Appropriation	6	7.3	*
House of Representatives			
001-10-0488 Congressional Use of Foreign Currency, House of Representatives			
Nondefense Mandatory Appropriation	1	7.3	*
Architect of the Capitol			
001-15-4518 Judiciary Office Building Development and Operations Fund			
Nondefense Mandatory Borrowing authority	12	7.3	1
Government Printing Office			
001-30-4505 Government Printing Office Revolving Fund			
Nondefense Mandatory Administrative expenses in otherwise exempt resources	2	7.3	*
Judicial Branch			
Courts of Appeals, District Courts, and other Judicial Services			
002-25-0920 Salaries and Expenses			
Nondefense Mandatory Appropriation	69	7.3	5
002-25-5100 Judiciary Filing Fees			
Nondefense Mandatory Appropriation	268	7.3	20
002-25-5101 Registry Administration			
Nondefense Mandatory Appropriation	1	7.3	*
Department of Agriculture			
Agricultural Research Service			
005-18-8214 Miscellaneous Contributed Funds			
Nondefense Mandatory Administrative expenses in otherwise exempt resources	2	7.3	*
National Institute of Food and Agriculture			
005-20-0502 Extension Activities			
Nondefense Mandatory Appropriation	5	7.3	*
Animal and Plant Health Inspection Service			
005-32-1600 Salaries and Expenses			
Nondefense Mandatory Appropriation	261	7.3	19
005-32-9971 Miscellaneous Trust Funds			
Nondefense Mandatory Administrative expenses in otherwise exempt resources	1	7.3	*
Food Safety and Inspection Service			
005-35-8137 Expenses and Refunds, Inspection and Grading of Farm Products			
Nondefense Mandatory Administrative expenses in otherwise exempt resources	1	7.3	*

* denotes amounts less than $500,000

Direct Spending Sequestrable Budgetary Resources and Reductions by Budget Account – FY 2014

(Amounts in millions)

Agency / Bureau / Account / Function / BEA Category / Budgetary Resource	Sequestrable BA Amount	Sequester Percentage	Sequester Amount
Department of Agriculture			
Grain Inspection, Packers and Stockyards Administration			
005-37-4050 Limitation on Inspection and Weighing Services Expenses			
Nondefense Mandatory Administrative expenses in otherwise exempt resources	1	7.3	*
Nondefense Mandatory Spending authority	40	7.3	3
Account Total	41		3
Agricultural Marketing Service			
005-45-5070 Perishable Agricultural Commodities Act Fund			
Nondefense Mandatory Appropriation	11	7.3	1
005-45-5209 Funds for Strengthening Markets, Income, and Supply (section 32)			
Nondefense Mandatory Appropriation	1,107	7.3	81
005-45-8015 Expenses and Refunds, Inspection and Grading of Farm Products			
Nondefense Mandatory Administrative expenses in otherwise exempt resources	4	7.3	*
Nondefense Mandatory Appropriation	8	7.3	1
Account Total	12		1
005-45-8412 Milk Market Orders Assessment Fund			
Nondefense Mandatory Spending authority	58	7.3	4
Risk Management Agency			
005-47-4085 Federal Crop Insurance Corporation Fund			
Nondefense Mandatory Administrative expenses in otherwise exempt resources	58	7.3	4
Farm Service Agency			
005-49-4336 Commodity Credit Corporation Fund			
Nondefense Mandatory Borrowing authority	7,968	7.3	582
005-49-8161 Tobacco Trust Fund			
Nondefense Mandatory Appropriation	960	7.3	70
Natural Resources Conservation Service			
005-53-1002 Watershed Rehabilitation Program			
Nondefense Mandatory Appropriation	165	7.3	12
005-53-1004 Farm Security and Rural Investment Programs			
Nondefense Mandatory Administrative expenses in otherwise exempt resources	96	7.3	7
Nondefense Mandatory Appropriation	3,558	7.3	260
Account Total	3,654		267
Rural Business_Cooperative Service			
005-65-1908 Rural Energy for America Program			
Nondefense Mandatory Appropriation	41	7.3	3
005-65-1955 Rural Microenterprise Investment Program Account			
Nondefense Mandatory Appropriation	3	7.3	*
005-65-2073 Energy Assistance Payments			
Nondefense Mandatory Appropriation	45	7.3	3
Foreign Agricultural Service			
005-68-2900 Salaries and Expenses			
Nondefense Mandatory Appropriation	2	7.3	*

* denotes amounts less than $500,000

Direct Spending Sequestrable Budgetary Resources and Reductions by Budget Account – FY 2014

(Amounts in millions)

Agency / Bureau / Account / Function / BEA Category / Budgetary Resource	Sequestrable BA Amount	Sequester Percentage	Sequester Amount
Department of Agriculture			
Food and Nutrition Service			
005-84-3505 Supplemental Nutrition Assistance Program			
Nondefense Mandatory Administrative expenses in otherwise exempt resources	111	7.3	8
005-84-3507 Commodity Assistance Program			
Nondefense Mandatory Appropriation	21	7.3	2
005-84-3510 Special Supplemental Nutrition Program for Women, Infants, and Children (WIC)			
Nondefense Mandatory Appropriation	1	7.3	*
005-84-3539 Child Nutrition Programs			
Nondefense Mandatory Administrative expenses in otherwise exempt resources	47	7.3	3
Nondefense Mandatory Appropriation	11	7.3	1
Account Total	58		4
Forest Service			
005-96-9921 Forest Service Permanent Appropriations			
Nondefense Mandatory Administrative expenses in otherwise exempt resources	1	7.3	*
Nondefense Mandatory Appropriation	245	7.3	18
Account Total	246		18
005-96-9923 Land Acquisition			
Nondefense Mandatory Appropriation	22	7.3	2
005-96-9974 Forest Service Trust Funds			
Nondefense Mandatory Administrative expenses in otherwise exempt resources	2	7.3	*
Nondefense Mandatory Appropriation	107	7.3	8
Account Total	109		8
Department of Commerce			
Departmental Management			
006-05-8501 Gifts and Bequests			
Nondefense Mandatory Administrative expenses in otherwise exempt resources	1	7.3	*
Bureau of the Census			
006-07-0401 Salaries and Expenses			
Nondefense Mandatory Appropriation	30	7.3	2
International Trade Administration			
006-25-5521 Grants to Manufacturers of Worsted Wool Fabrics			
Nondefense Mandatory Appropriation	5	7.3	*

* denotes amounts less than $500,000

Direct Spending Sequestrable Budgetary Resources and Reductions by Budget Account – FY 2014

(Amounts in millions)

Agency / Bureau / Account / Function / BEA Category / Budgetary Resource	Sequestrable BA Amount	Sequester Percentage	Sequester Amount
Department of Commerce			
National Oceanic and Atmospheric Administration			
006-48-4316 Damage Assessment and Restoration Revolving Fund			
Nondefense Mandatory Appropriation	8	7.3	1
006-48-5139 Promote and Develop Fishery Products and Research Pertaining to American Fisheries			
Nondefense Mandatory Appropriation	132	7.3	10
006-48-5284 Limited Access System Administration Fund			
Nondefense Mandatory Appropriation	10	7.3	1
006-48-5362 Environmental Improvement and Restoration Fund			
Nondefense Mandatory Appropriation	10	7.3	1
006-48-5583 Fisheries Enforcement Asset Forfeiture Fund			
Nondefense Mandatory Appropriation	5	7.3	*
006-48-5584 Sanctuaries Enforcement Asset Forfeiture Fund			
Nondefense Mandatory Appropriation	1	7.3	*
National Telecommunications and Information Administration			
006-60-8233 Public Safety Trust Fund			
Nondefense Mandatory Borrowing authority	1,908	7.3	139
Department of Defense--Military Programs			
Military Personnel			
007-05-0041 Concurrent Receipt Accrual Payments to the Military Retirement Fund			
Defense Mandatory Appropriation	6,970	9.8	683
Operation and Maintenance			
007-10-9922 Miscellaneous Special Funds			
Defense Mandatory Unobligated balance in 050	20	9.8	2
Family Housing			
007-30-0834 Department of Defense Family Housing Improvement Fund			
Defense Mandatory Unobligated balance in 050	76	9.8	7
Revolving and Management Funds			
007-40-4555 National Defense Stockpile Transaction Fund			
Defense Mandatory Spending authority	152	9.8	15
Defense Mandatory Unobligated balance in 050	320	9.8	31
Account Total	472		46
Trust Funds			
007-55-8164 Surcharge Collections, Sales of Commissary Stores, Defense			
Defense Mandatory Administrative expenses in otherwise exempt resources	217	9.8	21
007-55-9971 Other DOD Trust Funds			
Defense Mandatory Appropriation	26	9.8	3
Defense Mandatory Unobligated balance in 050	42	9.8	4
Account Total	68		7

* denotes amounts less than $500,000

Direct Spending Sequestrable Budgetary Resources and Reductions by Budget Account – FY 2014

(Amounts in millions)

Agency / Bureau / Account / Function / BEA Category / Budgetary Resource			Sequestrable BA Amount	Sequester Percentage	Sequester Amount
Department of Education					
Office of Special Education and Rehabilitative Services					
018-20-0301 Rehabilitation Services and Disability Research					
Nondefense	Mandatory	Appropriation	3,302	7.3	241
Office of Postsecondary Education					
018-40-0201 Higher Education					
Nondefense	Mandatory	Appropriation	428	7.3	31
Office of Federal Student Aid					
018-45-0200 Student Financial Assistance					
Nondefense	Mandatory	Appropriation	0	7.3	*
018-45-0202 Student Aid Administration					
Nondefense	Mandatory	Appropriation	434	7.3	32
018-45-0206 Teacher Education Assistance					
Nondefense	Mandatory	Appropriation	2	7.3	*
018-45-5557 Student Financial Assistance Debt Collection					
Nondefense	Mandatory	Appropriation	9	7.3	1
Department of Energy					
Energy Programs					
019-20-5105 Payments to States under Federal Power Act					
Nondefense	Mandatory	Appropriation	3	7.3	*
019-20-5523 Ultra-deepwater and Unconventional Natural Gas and Other Petroleum Research Fund					
Nondefense	Mandatory	Appropriation	50	7.3	4
Power Marketing Administration					
019-50-4045 Bonneville Power Administration Fund					
Nondefense	Mandatory	Administrative expenses in otherwise exempt resources	119	7.3	9
019-50-4404 Western Area Power Administration, Borrowing Authority, Recovery Act.					
Nondefense	Mandatory	Borrowing authority	29	7.3	2
Department of Health and Human Services					
Food and Drug Administration					
009-10-4309 Revolving Fund for Certification and Other Services					
Nondefense	Mandatory	Spending authority	8	7.3	1
Health Resources and Services Administration					
009-15-0321 Maternal, Infant, and Early Childhood Home Visiting Programs					
Nondefense	Mandatory	Appropriation	400	7.3	29
009-15-0350 Health Resources and Services					
Nondefense	Mandatory	Appropriation	522	7.3	38
Nondefense	Mandatory	Appropriation	1,983	2.0	40
Nondefense	Mandatory	Spending authority	16	7.3	1
		Account Total	2,521		79

* denotes amounts less than $500,000

Direct Spending Sequestrable Budgetary Resources and Reductions by Budget Account – FY 2014

(Amounts in millions)

Agency / Bureau / Account / Function / BEA Category / Budgetary Resource			Sequestrable BA Amount	Sequester Percentage	Sequester Amount
Department of Health and Human Services					
Indian Health Service					
009-17-0390 Indian Health Services					
Nondefense	Mandatory	Appropriation	150	2.0	3
Centers for Disease Control and Prevention					
009-20-0943 CDC-Wide Activities and Program Support					
Defense	Mandatory	Appropriation	55	9.8	5
009-20-0946 World Trade Center Health Program Fund					
Nondefense	Mandatory	Appropriation	267	7.3	19
National Institutes of Health					
009-25-9915 National Institutes of Health					
Nondefense	Mandatory	Appropriation	150	7.3	11
Centers for Medicare and Medicaid Services					
009-38-0115 Affordable Insurance Exchange Grants					
Nondefense	Mandatory	Appropriation	1,343	7.3	98
009-38-0126 Reduced Cost Sharing for Individuals Enrolling in Qualified Health Plans					
Nondefense	Mandatory	Appropriation	3,978	7.3	290
009-38-0511 Program Management					
Nondefense	Mandatory	Appropriation	253	7.3	18
Nondefense	Mandatory	Spending authority	944	7.3	69
		Account Total	1,197		87
009-38-0516 State Grants and Demonstrations					
Nondefense	Mandatory	Appropriation	532	7.3	39
009-38-8004 Federal Supplementary Medical Insurance Trust Fund					
Nondefense	Mandatory	Appropriation	253,692	2.0	5,074
Nondefense	Mandatory	Appropriation	163	7.3	12
		Account Total	253,855		5,086
009-38-8005 Federal Hospital Insurance Trust Fund					
Nondefense	Mandatory	Appropriation	696	7.3	51
Nondefense	Mandatory	Appropriation	277,944	2.0	5,559
		Account Total	278,640		5,610
009-38-8308 Medicare Prescription Drug Account, Federal Supplementary Insurance Trust Fund					
Nondefense	Mandatory	Appropriation	25,651	2.0	513
Nondefense	Mandatory	Appropriation	4	7.3	*
		Account Total	25,655		513
009-38-8393 Health Care Fraud and Abuse Control Account					
Nondefense	Mandatory	Appropriation	508	7.3	37
Nondefense	Mandatory	Appropriation	812	2.0	16
		Account Total	1,320		53

* denotes amounts less than $500,000

Direct Spending Sequestrable Budgetary Resources and Reductions by Budget Account – FY 2014

(Amounts in millions)

Agency / Bureau / Account / Function / BEA Category / Budgetary Resource	Sequestrable BA Amount	Sequester Percentage	Sequester Amount
Department of Health and Human Services			
Administration for Children and Families			
009-70-1501 Payments to States for Child Support Enforcement and Family Support Programs			
Nondefense Mandatory Appropriation	1	7.3	*
009-70-1512 Supporting Healthy Families and Adolescent Development			
Nondefense Mandatory Appropriation	470	7.3	34
009-70-1534 Social Services Block Grant			
Nondefense Mandatory Appropriation	1,785	7.3	130
009-70-1545 Payments for Foster Care and Permanency			
Nondefense Mandatory Administrative expenses in otherwise exempt resources	2	7.3	*
009-70-1552 Temporary Assistance for Needy Families			
Nondefense Mandatory Administrative expenses in otherwise exempt resources	26	7.3	2
009-70-1553 Children's Research and Technical Assistance			
Nondefense Mandatory Appropriation	52	7.3	4
Nondefense Mandatory Spending authority	1	7.3	*
Account Total	53		4
Administration for Community Living			
009-75-0142 Aging and Disability Services Programs			
Nondefense Mandatory Appropriation	10	7.3	1
Departmental Management			
009-90-0116 Prevention and Public Health Fund			
Nondefense Mandatory Appropriation	1,000	7.3	73
009-90-0117 Pregnancy Assistance Fund			
Nondefense Mandatory Appropriation	25	7.3	2
Program Support Center			
009-91-9971 Miscellaneous Trust Funds			
Nondefense Mandatory Administrative expenses in otherwise exempt resources	47	7.3	3
Office of the Inspector General			
009-92-0128 Office of the Inspector General			
Nondefense Mandatory Spending authority	12	7.3	1
Department of Homeland Security			
Citizenship and Immigration Services			
024-30-0300 Citizenship and Immigration Services			
Nondefense Mandatory Appropriation	3,095	7.3	226
Nondefense Mandatory Spending authority	6	7.3	*
Account Total	3,101		226
Transportation Security Administration			
024-45-0550 Aviation Security			
Nondefense Mandatory Appropriation	250	7.3	18
024-45-0557 Transportation Threat Assessment and Credentialing			
Nondefense Mandatory Spending authority	5	7.3	*

* denotes amounts less than $500,000

Direct Spending Sequestrable Budgetary Resources and Reductions by Budget Account – FY 2014

(Amounts in millions)

Agency / Bureau / Account / Function / BEA Category / Budgetary Resource	Sequestrable BA Amount	Sequester Percentage	Sequester Amount
Department of Homeland Security			
Immigration and Customs Enforcement			
024-55-0540 Immigration and Customs Enforcement			
Nondefense Mandatory Appropriation	690	7.3	50
Customs and Border Protection			
024-58-0530 Customs and Border Protection			
Nondefense Mandatory Appropriation	1,498	7.3	109
024-58-5533 Payments to Wool Manufacturers			
Nondefense Mandatory Appropriation	15	7.3	1
024-58-5595 Electronic System for Travel Authorization			
Nondefense Mandatory Appropriation	55	7.3	4
024-58-5687 Refunds, Transfers, and Expenses of Operation, Puerto Rico			
Nondefense Mandatory Appropriation	99	7.3	7
024-58-8789 U.S. Customs Refunds, Transfers and Expenses, Unclaimed and Abandoned Goods			
Nondefense Mandatory Appropriation	4	7.3	*
United States Coast Guard			
024-60-8149 Boat Safety			
Nondefense Mandatory Appropriation	109	7.3	8
024-60-8349 Maritime Oil Spill Programs			
Nondefense Mandatory Appropriation	239	7.3	17
Federal Emergency Management Agency			
024-70-4236 National Flood Insurance Fund			
Nondefense Mandatory Administrative expenses in otherwise exempt resources	2,122	7.3	155
Department of Housing and Urban Development			
Housing Programs			
025-09-4041 Rental Housing Assistance Fund			
Nondefense Mandatory Spending authority	3	7.3	*
Department of the Interior			
Bureau of Land Management			
010-04-5132 Range Improvements			
Nondefense Mandatory Appropriation	10	7.3	1
010-04-9921 Miscellaneous Permanent Payment Accounts			
Nondefense Mandatory Appropriation	14	7.3	1
010-04-9926 Permanent Operating Funds			
Nondefense Mandatory Appropriation	35	7.3	3
010-04-9971 Miscellaneous Trust Funds			
Nondefense Mandatory Administrative expenses in otherwise exempt resources	22	7.3	2

* denotes amounts less than $500,000

Direct Spending Sequestrable Budgetary Resources and Reductions by Budget Account – FY 2014

(Amounts in millions)

Agency / Bureau / Account / Function / BEA Category / Budgetary Resource	Sequestrable BA Amount	Sequester Percentage	Sequester Amount
Department of the Interior			
Office of Surface Mining Reclamation and Enforcement			
010-08-1803 Payments to States in Lieu of Coal Fee Receipts			
Nondefense Mandatory Appropriation	128	7.3	9
010-08-5015 Abandoned Mine Reclamation Fund			
Nondefense Mandatory Appropriation	188	7.3	14
Bureau of Reclamation			
010-10-0680 Water and Related Resources			
Nondefense Mandatory Appropriation	1	7.3	*
010-10-4079 Lower Colorado River Basin Development Fund			
Nondefense Mandatory Administrative expenses in otherwise exempt resources	5	7.3	*
Nondefense Mandatory Spending authority	1	7.3	*
Account Total	6		0
010-10-4081 Upper Colorado River Basin Fund			
Nondefense Mandatory Administrative expenses in otherwise exempt resources	3	7.3	*
010-10-5656 Colorado River Dam Fund, Boulder Canyon Project			
Nondefense Mandatory Administrative expenses in otherwise exempt resources	8	7.3	1
010-10-8070 Reclamation Trust Funds			
Nondefense Mandatory Administrative expenses in otherwise exempt resources	1	7.3	*
Central Utah Project			
010-11-5174 Utah Reclamation Mitigation and Conservation Account			
Nondefense Mandatory Appropriation	7	7.3	1
United States Fish and Wildlife Service			
010-18-5029 Federal Aid in Wildlife Restoration			
Nondefense Mandatory Appropriation	611	7.3	45
010-18-5091 National Wildlife Refuge Fund			
Nondefense Mandatory Appropriation	8	7.3	1
010-18-5137 Migratory Bird Conservation Account			
Nondefense Mandatory Appropriation	52	7.3	4
010-18-5241 North American Wetlands Conservation Fund			
Nondefense Mandatory Appropriation	1	7.3	*
010-18-5252 Recreation Enhancement Fee Program, FWS			
Nondefense Mandatory Administrative expenses in otherwise exempt resources	1	7.3	*
010-18-8151 Sport Fish Restoration			
Nondefense Mandatory Appropriation	421	7.3	31

* denotes amounts less than $500,000

Direct Spending Sequestrable Budgetary Resources and Reductions by Budget Account – FY 2014

(Amounts in millions)

Agency / Bureau / Account / Function / BEA Category / Budgetary Resource	Sequestrable BA Amount	Sequester Percentage	Sequester Amount
Department of the Interior			
National Park Service			
010-24-5035 Land Acquisition and State Assistance			
Nondefense Mandatory Contract authority	30	7.3	2
010-24-9924 Other Permanent Appropriations			
Nondefense Mandatory Administrative expenses in otherwise exempt resources	8	7.3	1
010-24-9928 Recreation Fee Permanent Appropriations			
Nondefense Mandatory Administrative expenses in otherwise exempt resources	35	7.3	3
Nondefense Mandatory Appropriation	1	7.3	*
Account Total	36		3
Bureau of Indian Affairs and Bureau of Indian Education			
010-76-5051 Operation and Maintenance of Quarters			
Nondefense Mandatory Administrative expenses in otherwise exempt resources	3	7.3	*
010-76-9925 Miscellaneous Permanent Appropriations			
Nondefense Mandatory Administrative expenses in otherwise exempt resources	19	7.3	1
Departmental Offices			
010-84-5003 Mineral Leasing and Associated Payments			
Nondefense Mandatory Appropriation	2,142	7.3	156
010-84-5045 National Petroleum Reserve, Alaska			
Nondefense Mandatory Appropriation	3	7.3	*
010-84-5243 National Forests Fund, Payment to States			
Nondefense Mandatory Appropriation	8	7.3	1
010-84-5248 Leases of Lands Acquired for Flood Control, Navigation, and Allied Purposes			
Nondefense Mandatory Appropriation	27	7.3	2
010-84-5535 States Share from Certain Gulf of Mexico Leases			
Nondefense Mandatory Appropriation	3	7.3	*
010-84-5574 Geothermal Lease Revenues, Payment to Counties			
Nondefense Mandatory Appropriation	4	7.3	*
Insular Affairs			
010-85-0412 Assistance to Territories			
Nondefense Mandatory Administrative expenses in otherwise exempt resources	9	7.3	1
National Indian Gaming Commission			
010-92-5141 National Indian Gaming Commission, Gaming Activity Fees			
Nondefense Mandatory Appropriation	19	7.3	1
Department-Wide Programs			
010-95-1618 Natural Resource Damage Assessment Fund			
Nondefense Mandatory Administrative expenses in otherwise exempt resources	8	7.3	1

* denotes amounts less than $500,000

Direct Spending Sequestrable Budgetary Resources and Reductions by Budget Account – FY 2014

(Amounts in millions)

Agency / Bureau / Account / Function / BEA Category / Budgetary Resource			Sequestrable BA Amount	Sequester Percentage	Sequester Amount
Department of Justice					
Legal Activities and U.S. Marshals					
011-05-0311 Fees and Expenses of Witnesses					
Nondefense	Mandatory	Appropriation	270	7.3	20
011-05-0340 September 11th Victim Compensation					
Nondefense	Mandatory	Appropriation	200	7.3	15
011-05-5042 Assets Forfeiture Fund					
Nondefense	Mandatory	Appropriation	2,163	7.3	158
Drug Enforcement Administration					
011-12-5131 Diversion Control Fee Account					
Nondefense	Mandatory	Appropriation	356	7.3	26
Federal Prison System					
011-20-8408 Commissary Funds, Federal Prisons					
Nondefense	Mandatory	Administrative expenses in otherwise exempt resources	111	7.3	8
Office of Justice Programs					
011-21-0403 Public Safety Officer Benefits					
Nondefense	Mandatory	Administrative expenses in otherwise exempt resources	1	7.3	*
011-21-5041 Crime Victims Fund					
Nondefense	Mandatory	Appropriation	800	7.3	58
Department of Labor					
Employment and Training Administration					
012-05-0168 Short Time Compensation Programs					
Nondefense	Mandatory	Appropriation	215	7.3	16
012-05-0174 Training and Employment Services					
Nondefense	Mandatory	Appropriation	125	7.3	9
012-05-0179 State Unemployment Insurance and Employment Service Operations					
Nondefense	Mandatory	Appropriation	13	7.3	1
012-05-0187 TAA Community College and Career Training Grant Fund					
Nondefense	Mandatory	Appropriation	500	7.3	37
012-05-0326 Federal Unemployment Benefits and Allowances					
Nondefense	Mandatory	Appropriation	978	7.3	71
012-05-8042 Unemployment Trust Fund					
Nondefense	Mandatory	Administrative expenses in otherwise exempt resources	90	7.3	7
Nondefense	Mandatory	Appropriation	7,828	7.3	571
		Account Total	7,918		578
Pension Benefit Guaranty Corporation					
012-12-4204 Pension Benefit Guaranty Corporation Fund					
Nondefense	Mandatory	Administrative expenses in otherwise exempt resources	122	7.3	9

* denotes amounts less than $500,000

Direct Spending Sequestrable Budgetary Resources and Reductions by Budget Account – FY 2014

(Amounts in millions)

Agency / Bureau / Account / Function / BEA Category / Budgetary Resource	Sequestrable BA Amount	Sequester Percentage	Sequester Amount
Department of Labor			
Office of Workers' Compensation Programs			
012-15-0169 Special Benefits for Disabled Coal Miners			
Nondefense Mandatory Administrative expenses in otherwise exempt resources	5	7.3	*
012-15-1524 Administrative Expenses, Energy Employees Occupational Illness Compensation Fund			
Defense Mandatory Appropriation	129	9.8	13
Defense Mandatory Unobligated balance in 050	6	9.8	1
Account Total	135		14
012-15-8144 Black Lung Disability Trust Fund			
Nondefense Mandatory Administrative expenses in otherwise exempt resources	59	7.3	4
Wage and Hour Division			
012-16-5393 H-1 B and L Fraud Prevention and Detection			
Nondefense Mandatory Appropriation	35	7.3	3
Department of State			
Administration of Foreign Affairs			
014-05-0113 Diplomatic and Consular Programs			
Nondefense Mandatory Appropriation	41	7.3	3
Department of Transportation			
Office of the Secretary			
021-04-5423 Essential Air Service and Rural Airport Improvement Fund			
Nondefense Mandatory Appropriation	116	7.3	8
Federal Aviation Administration			
021-12-4120 Aviation Insurance Revolving Fund			
Nondefense Mandatory Administrative expenses in otherwise exempt resources	2	7.3	*
Federal Highway Administration			
021-15-0534 Payment to the Transportation Trust Fund			
Nondefense Mandatory Appropriation	12,600	7.3	920
021-15-8083 Federal-aid Highways			
Nondefense Mandatory Contract authority	739	7.3	54
Pipeline and Hazardous Materials Safety Administration			
021-50-5282 Emergency Preparedness Grants			
Nondefense Mandatory Appropriation	28	7.3	2
Maritime Administration			
021-70-1751 Ocean Freight Differential			
Nondefense Mandatory Borrowing authority	100	7.3	7

* denotes amounts less than $500,000

Direct Spending Sequestrable Budgetary Resources and Reductions by Budget Account – FY 2014

(Amounts in millions)

Agency / Bureau / Account / Function / BEA Category / Budgetary Resource	Sequestrable BA Amount	Sequester Percentage	Sequester Amount
Department of the Treasury			
Departmental Offices			
015-05-0123 Terrorism Insurance Program			
Nondefense Mandatory Administrative expenses in otherwise exempt resources	3	7.3	*
015-05-0126 GSE Mortgage-Backed Securities Purchase Program Account			
Nondefense Mandatory Appropriation	10	7.3	1
015-05-0140 Grants for Specified Energy Property in Lieu of Tax Credits, Recovery Act			
Nondefense Mandatory Appropriation	4,710	7.3	344
015-05-0141 Small Business Lending Fund Program Account			
Nondefense Mandatory Appropriation	20	7.3	1
015-05-5081 Presidential Election Campaign Fund			
Nondefense Mandatory Appropriation	33	7.3	2
015-05-5590 Financial Research Fund			
Nondefense Mandatory Appropriation	113	7.3	8
015-05-5697 Treasury Forfeiture Fund			
Nondefense Mandatory Appropriation	1,544	7.3	113
Fiscal Service			
015-12-0520 Salaries and Expenses, Fiscal Service			
Nondefense Mandatory Administrative expenses in otherwise exempt resources	12	7.3	1
015-12-1710 Payment of Government Losses in Shipment			
Nondefense Mandatory Appropriation	1	7.3	*
015-12-5688 Continued Dumping and Subsidy Offset			
Nondefense Mandatory Appropriation	100	7.3	7
015-12-8209 Cheyenne River Sioux Tribe Terrestrial Wildlife Habitat Restoration Trust Fund			
Nondefense Mandatory Appropriation	2	7.3	*
015-12-8625 Gulf Coast Restoration Trust Fund			
Nondefense Mandatory Appropriation	320	7.3	23
015-12-8626 Santee Sioux Tribe Development Trust Fund			
Nondefense Mandatory Appropriation	4	7.3	*
015-12-8627 Yankton Sioux Tribe Development Trust Fund			
Nondefense Mandatory Appropriation	18	7.3	1

* denotes amounts less than $500,000

Direct Spending Sequestrable Budgetary Resources and Reductions by Budget Account – FY 2014

(Amounts in millions)

Agency / Bureau / Account / Function / BEA Category / Budgetary Resource	Sequestrable BA Amount	Sequester Percentage	Sequester Amount
Department of the Treasury			
Internal Revenue Service			
015-45-0935 Build America Bond Payments, Recovery Act			
Nondefense Mandatory Appropriation	4,334	7.3	316
015-45-0945 Payment to Issuer of Qualified Zone Academy Bonds			
Nondefense Mandatory Appropriation	38	7.3	3
015-45-0946 Payment to Issuer of Qualified School Construction Bonds			
Nondefense Mandatory Appropriation	820	7.3	60
015-45-0947 Payment to Issuer of New Clean Renewable Energy Bonds			
Nondefense Mandatory Appropriation	24	7.3	2
015-45-0948 Payment to Issuer of Qualified Energy Conservation Bonds			
Nondefense Mandatory Appropriation	32	7.3	2
015-45-0951 Payment Where Small Business Health Insurance Tax Credit Exceeds Liability for Tax			
Nondefense Mandatory Appropriation	140	7.3	10
015-45-0952 Therapeutic Discovery Program Grants and Administration			
Nondefense Mandatory Appropriation	2	7.3	*
015-45-5432 IRS Miscellaneous Retained Fees			
Nondefense Mandatory Appropriation	39	7.3	3
015-45-5433 Informant Payments			
Nondefense Mandatory Appropriation	125	7.3	9
Corps of Engineers--Civil Works			
202-00-4902 Revolving Fund			
Nondefense Mandatory Administrative expenses in otherwise exempt resources	36	7.3	3
202-00-8217 South Dakota Terrestrial Wildlife Habitat Restoration Trust Fund			
Nondefense Mandatory Appropriation	4	7.3	*
202-00-8333 Coastal Wetlands Restoration Trust Fund			
Nondefense Mandatory Appropriation	77	7.3	6
202-00-8862 Rivers and Harbors Contributed Funds			
Nondefense Mandatory Administrative expenses in otherwise exempt resources	104	7.3	8
202-00-9921 Permanent Appropriations			
Nondefense Mandatory Appropriation	20	7.3	1
Environmental Protection Agency			
020-00-4310 Reregistration and Expedited Processing Revolving Fund			
Nondefense Mandatory Spending authority	28	7.3	2
020-00-8145 Hazardous Substance Superfund			
Nondefense Mandatory Appropriation	19	7.3	1
General Services Administration			
Real Property Activities			
023-05-5254 Disposal of Surplus Real and Related Personal Property			
Nondefense Mandatory Appropriation	9	7.3	1

* denotes amounts less than $500,000

Direct Spending Sequestrable Budgetary Resources and Reductions by Budget Account – FY 2014

(Amounts in millions)

Agency / Bureau / Account / Function / BEA Category / Budgetary Resource	Sequestrable BA Amount	Sequester Percentage	Sequester Amount
General Services Administration			
Supply and Technology Activities			
023-10-5250 Expenses of Transportation Audit Contracts and Contract Administration			
Nondefense Mandatory Appropriation	12	7.3	1
International Assistance Programs			
Military Sales Program			
184-70-8242 Foreign Military Sales Trust Fund			
Nondefense Mandatory Administrative expenses in otherwise exempt resources	147	7.3	11
National Aeronautics and Space Administration			
026-00-8978 Science, Space, and Technology Education Trust Fund			
Nondefense Mandatory Appropriation	1	7.3	*
National Science Foundation			
422-00-0106 Education and Human Resources			
Nondefense Mandatory Appropriation	100	7.3	7
422-00-8960 Donations			
Nondefense Mandatory Administrative expenses in otherwise exempt resources	16	7.3	1
Office of Personnel Management			
027-00-0800 Flexible Benefits Plan Reserve			
Nondefense Mandatory Spending authority	30	7.3	2
027-00-8135 Civil Service Retirement and Disability Fund			
Nondefense Mandatory Administrative expenses in otherwise exempt resources	48	7.3	4
027-00-8424 Employees Life Insurance Fund			
Nondefense Mandatory Administrative expenses in otherwise exempt resources	2	7.3	*
Affordable Housing Program			
530-00-5528 Affordable Housing Program			
Nondefense Mandatory Appropriation	286	7.3	21
Appalachian Regional Commission			
309-00-9971 Miscellaneous Trust Funds			
Nondefense Mandatory Appropriation	9	7.3	1
Bureau of Consumer Financial Protection			
581-00-5577 Bureau of Consumer Financial Protection Fund			
Nondefense Mandatory Appropriation	497	7.3	36
Commodity Futures Trading Commission			
339-00-4334 Customer Protection Fund			
Nondefense Mandatory Spending authority	12	7.3	1

* denotes amounts less than $500,000

Direct Spending Sequestrable Budgetary Resources and Reductions by Budget Account – FY 2014

(Amounts in millions)

Agency / Bureau / Account / Function / BEA Category / Budgetary Resource	Sequestrable BA Amount	Sequester Percentage	Sequester Amount
Corporation for Travel Promotion			
580-00-5585 Travel Promotion Fund			
Nondefense Mandatory Appropriation	100	7.3	7
District of Columbia			
District of Columbia Courts			
349-10-8212 District of Columbia Judicial Retirement and Survivors Annuity Fund			
Nondefense Mandatory Administrative expenses in otherwise exempt resources	1	7.3	*
District of Columbia General and Special Payments			
349-30-5511 District of Columbia Federal Pension Fund			
Nondefense Mandatory Administrative expenses in otherwise exempt resources	17	7.3	1
Electric Reliability Organization			
531-00-5522 Electric Reliability Organization			
Nondefense Mandatory Appropriation	100	7.3	7
Equal Employment Opportunity Commission			
350-00-4019 EEOC Education, Technical Assistance, and Training Revolving Fund			
Nondefense Mandatory Administrative expenses in otherwise exempt resources	4	7.3	*
Farm Credit System Insurance Corporation			
355-00-4171 Farm Credit System Insurance Fund			
Nondefense Mandatory Administrative expenses in otherwise exempt resources	4	7.3	*
Federal Communications Commission			
356-00-0300 Spectrum Auction Program Account			
Nondefense Mandatory Appropriation	2	7.3	*
356-00-5610 TV Broadcaster Relocation Fund			
Nondefense Mandatory Borrowing authority	500	7.3	37
Federal Deposit Insurance Corporation			
Orderly Liquidation			
357-35-5586 Orderly Liquidation Fund			
Nondefense Mandatory Appropriation	158	7.3	12
Nondefense Mandatory Borrowing authority	1,410	7.3	103
Account Total	1,568		115
Federal Financial Institutions Examination Council			
Federal Financial Institutions Examination Council Appraisal Subcommittee			
362-20-5026 Registry Fees			
Nondefense Mandatory Appropriation	3	7.3	*

* denotes amounts less than $500,000

Direct Spending Sequestrable Budgetary Resources and Reductions by Budget Account – FY 2014

(Amounts in millions)

Agency / Bureau / Account / Function / BEA Category / Budgetary Resource	Sequestrable BA Amount	Sequester Percentage	Sequester Amount
Morris K. Udall and Stewart L. Udall Foundation			
487-00-5415 Environmental Dispute Resolution Fund			
Nondefense Mandatory Administrative expenses in otherwise exempt resources	4	7.3	*
National Archives and Records Administration			
393-00-8436 National Archives Trust Fund			
Nondefense Mandatory Administrative expenses in otherwise exempt resources	1	7.3	*
Patient-Centered Outcomes Research Trust Fund			
579-00-8299 Patient-Centered Outcomes Research Trust Fund			
Nondefense Mandatory Appropriation	623	7.3	45
Public Company Accounting Oversight Board			
526-00-5376 Public Company Accounting Oversight Board			
Nondefense Mandatory Appropriation	253	7.3	18
Railroad Retirement Board			
446-00-8051 Railroad Unemployment Insurance Trust Fund			
Nondefense Mandatory Appropriation	101	7.3	7
Nondefense Mandatory Spending authority	23	7.3	2
Account Total	124		9
Securities and Exchange Commission			
449-00-5566 Securities and Exchange Commission Reserve Fund			
Nondefense Mandatory Appropriation	75	7.3	5
449-00-5567 Investor Protection Fund			
Nondefense Mandatory Appropriation	90	7.3	7
Securities Investor Protection Corporation			
576-00-5600 Securities Investor Protection Corporation			
Nondefense Mandatory Appropriation	335	7.3	24
Standard Setting Body			
527-00-5377 Payment to Standard Setting Body			
Nondefense Mandatory Appropriation	30	7.3	2
Tennessee Valley Authority			
455-00-4110 Tennessee Valley Authority Fund			
Nondefense Mandatory Administrative expenses in otherwise exempt resources	455	7.3	33
Vietnam Education Foundation			
519-00-5365 Vietnam Debt Repayment Fund			
Nondefense Mandatory Appropriation	5	7.3	*

* denotes amounts less than $500,000

NOTES

Amounts may not sum to total due to rounding.

Mandatory Federal administrative expenses of otherwise exempt accounts are sequestrable pursuant to section 251A(8) and section 256(h) of BBEDCA.

Unobligated balances of budget authority carried over from prior fiscal years in defense function 050 accounts are sequestrable.

For intragovernmental payments, sequestration is applied to the paying account. The funds are generally exempt in the receiving account in accordance with section 255(g)(1)(A) of BBEDCA so that the same dollars are not sequestered twice.